Someone Wants to Die

S. J. Anderson

Help for People Struggling with Suicide

INTERVARSITY PRESS
DOWNERS GROVE, ILLINOIS 60515

For Charlotte, who tenaciously
helps me to choose life.

© *1988 by S. J. Anderson*

All rights reserved. No part of this book may be reproduced in any form without written permission from InterVarsity Press, P.O. Box 1400, Downers Grove, IL 60515.

InterVarsity Press is the book-publishing division of InterVarsity Christian Fellowship, a student movement active on campus at hundreds of universities, colleges and schools of nursing. For information about local and regional activities, write Public Relations Dept., InterVarsity Christian Fellowship, 6400 Schroeder Rd., P.O. Box 7895, Madison, WI 53707-7895.

Distributed in Canada through InterVarsity Press, 860 Denison St., Unit 3, Markham, Ontario L3R 4H1, Canada.

All Scripture quotations, unless otherwise indicated, are from the Holy Bible, New International Version. Copyright © 1973, 1978, International Bible Society. Used by permission of Zondervan Bible Publishers.

Cover photograph: Robert McKendrick

ISBN 0-87784-220-5

Printed in the United States of America

13	12	11	10	9	8	7	6	5	4	3	2	1
97	96	95	94	93	92	91	90	89	88			

One never knows what's inside another person.
Jesse Helms, on the suicide of his Senate colleague John East

---

O LORD, you have searched me and you know me.
Psalm 139:1

The closest I have come to killing myself was five years ago when I was thirty years old. It was two hours after I had lost a job with a Christian organization. I walked into my apartment and locked the door. Rather than running to the phone to call a friend, I shut all the curtains and pulled all the shades. I poured myself a glass of wine, went into the bedroom, locked the door and sat at my desk in the darkness I had come to know so well.

4

The peace I felt stunned me. I was no longer reaching out to death as much as it was reaching out to me. It whispered, *You aren't angry anymore. You're only tired. You want to sleep. You have enough pills to swallow so that you can lie down and sleep forever. You're so very tired.* The voice taunted me, comforted me. I remember laughing nervously as I stood up, took a deep breath and gathered the strength I would need to walk the fifteen feet separating me from the bathroom medicine cabinet.

Seeds of the Struggle

The first time I can remember wanting to end my life was when I was ten. Holding a copy of *Time* magazine, I looked deeply into the eyes of Lee Harvey Oswald on the cover and thought, *I can assassinate somebody famous. Then someone will shoot me.* I pasted his picture alongside pictures of Julius Caesar, Abraham Lincoln, John Wilkes Booth, John Kennedy and others in a special scrapbook I had begun about assassinations.

Through the years, my fascination with assassinations grew, as did my thoughts of suicide. In eighth grade, I received an *A* for creating a miniature replica of the stage area of Ford's Theater, where Lincoln was shot. Two years later, I retreated to the darkened high school auditorium before school one day and

5

cut my left wrist with my geometry compass. I bled enough to go to the nurse's office, but not enough to be sent home. I felt foolish and frightened that I was so desperate for attention. I prayed, *Will you forgive me, God, for being so selfish?*

When it was time for graduation, I ranked fourth out of a high school class of 214 and received the Danforth Foundation Leadership Award for "Outstanding Senior Girl." I was surprised to hear my school's faculty had chosen me; even though I didn't drink, smoke or take drugs, I had a reputation for being angry and rebellious. The faculty chairman said that I got the award for always asking, *Why?*

I never realized I did that until he told me. But he was right. I asked why all the time! *Why is the United States in Vietnam? Why were Martin Luther King, Jr., and Bobby Kennedy assassinated? Why were four students killed at Kent State?* But there were questions I asked myself, too: *Why do I feel so bad about these things? Why do I think life will always be this way? Why do I feel like such a failure? Why do I feel so lonely? Why do I want to die?* There were never answers.

Although I had been raised in a family that attended church regularly, I did not accept Christ as my personal Savior until I was twenty years old. The night I asked him into my life, I experienced the joy of knowing I would never again be alone. I chose to go to a Christian college, and I thought little about killing myself until my senior year. That year I edited the student newspaper, which soon became infamous for its sense of humor. My friends told me, "It just doesn't make sense that somebody so young, bright and funny should be so depressed." I wondered why no one knew I was using humor to help myself cling to life, to buy time to figure what sin had caused my feelings of loneliness and defeat.

I graduated *summa cum laude* from college and began a career in writing and editing in hopes that by working with words I could give my life some meaning. I kept busy with church activities, too, but most of the time I felt empty. Sometimes I thought that if I had a larger savings account or a house—a place to call my own—I would feel more secure about the future. Most often I wished for a terminal illness—cancer, perhaps—so that a doctor could hand me tangible lab results proving my body had betrayed me. Then I could look at the chart and say, "Now I know why I feel like I'm dying."

Therapists told me no, nothing seemed to indicate a psychotic disorder—only a depression that would diminish with time, hard work and anti-depressants. My friends, the ones who had not yet abandoned me in frustration, recommended books, prayer, community volunteer work and even exorcism.

Too many times I threatened to kill myself purely for attention—to get a friend to come over, listen for hours and hold me while I cried. Too many times that friend's comfort—like day-old manna—tasted like sawdust, and I felt even worse for having manipulated someone who so obviously cared for me.

So I spent more and more time alone, lying in bed. I began to dread the moment morning light would fill my eyes. Taunting me to rise out of bed, that light seemed to pin me like an insect, searing a hot hole through my heart, a heart I thought belonged to Jesus Christ. I felt powerless. I became afraid of God. With the psalmist in Psalm 88:14-18, I pleaded:

> Why, O Lord, do you reject me
> and hide your face from me?
> From my youth I have been afflicted
> and close to death;
> I have suffered your terrors and am in
> despair.
> Your wrath has swept over me;
> your terrors have destroyed me.
> All day long they surround me like a flood;
> they have completely engulfed me.
> You have taken my companions and loved
> ones from me;
> the darkness is my closest friend.

8

One day I received word that a Presbyterian pastor I knew had killed herself. They had found her body suspended from a living-room curtain rod. At the funeral home her coffin was left open. Looking at her face, still grimacing, I recalled a children's sermon she had preached about how God had the whole wide world in his hands. Now she was gone forever in those hands. As I stood there between two friends, my legs buckled beneath me. Would those same hands one day reach out and take me too?

In order to preserve my life, I became convinced that I had to stop praying, reading the Bible and going to church. I resolved to see my life objectively, through my own eyes and not the eyes of God. In my journal I made two lists. One was labeled *Reasons for Living*. Under it were *friends, writing, my cat, music, Lake Michigan* and *art*. The other was labeled *Reasons for Dying*. Under it were *feeling unloved; feeling abandoned; too expensive, financially and emotionally, to live; things will never change; I don't have the strength to become like Christ;* and *If I kill myself, I can immediately be in God's presence rather than waiting an agonizing lifetime*. This last reason hooked me. I suddenly had an incredible sense of security. I had power after all, if only to end my life. Yes, the darkness was my closest friend.

9

The Prevalence of Suicide

All of us at one time or another have wanted to die, if only in a passing thought on a particularly depressing day. A careless oversight sabotages years of work. A heartless comment ends a promising relationship. A devastating mental or physical illness eradicates our hope in God. Feeling powerless, we retreat to our beds, weeping bitterly and praying never again to see the light of day. Most people wake up the next morning knowing the world has not come to an end. They somehow gather the strength they need to walk through the despair. But some of us choose differently.

Once every minute, someone attempts to choose death over life—and some succeed. Worldwide, more than half a million people commit suicide every year, according to the World Health Organization. In the United States, more people die by suicide than by homicide. The eighth leading cause of death, suicide claims 30,000 victims annually. The real number could be as high as 100,000, some experts believe, because suicide often masquerades as automobile accidents, drug overdoses and eating disorders. Then, too, the families of victims often deny the death was self-destructive; they fear the social and religious stigmas attached to suicide. And for every successful suicide, there are at least eight to ten attempts.

Heightening this tragedy is the alarming three hundred per cent increase in adolescent suicide since 1955. Suicide now ranks as the third leading cause of death for Americans between the ages of fifteen and twenty-four, claiming as many as six thousand youths a year, according to the federal Centers for Disease Control in Atlanta. This year, an estimated two million young people between the ages of fifteen and nineteen will try to kill themselves.

Suicide knows no geographic, economic, social or religious boundaries. Without doubt, these statistics include many people who are Christians. How should Christians respond to an act that seemingly defies rational understanding, not to mention a God who embraces all life as sacred?

Why Do People Choose Death?

In his book, *The Savage God* (written after the suicide of his good friend, poet Sylvia Plath), A. Alvarez describes the elusive, mysterious power of suicide:

> [It is] a closed world, with its own irresistible logic. . . . It is like the unanswerable logic of a nightmare, or like the science fiction fantasy of being projected suddenly into another dimension: everything makes sense and follows its own strict rules; yet, at the

same time, everything is also different, perverted, upside down. Once a man decides to take his own life, he enters a shut-off, impregnable but wholly convincing world where every detail fits and each incident reinforces his decision.[1]

Why does a person enter—or even think of entering—such a dark, closed world? What in these people's lives set them apart?

☐ In June of 1986, Republican Senator John East committed suicide in the garage of his North Carolina home.

☐ A sixteen-year-old Boy Scout troop leader and honors student killed himself with his father's rifle.

☐ A twenty-five-year-old University of Wisconsin student, active in Christian ministry, swallowed nearly two bottles of aspirin and cut his wrists before lunging through a fourth-story dormitory window.

☐ A twenty-one-year-old champion distance-runner from North Carolina State University jumped from a bridge during the June 1986 NCAA championships, permanently paralyzing herself from the waist down. She had been valedictorian of her high school class of 600 and planned to become a medical missionary.

Newspaper accounts leave little or no clues to the motives behind such desperate acts. Although Senator East suffered from severe hypothyroidism, his press secretary stated that East "increasingly took on more work" and that his health problems "didn't seem to interfere."[2] The sixteen-year-old Boy Scout leader "left behind no note, no diary, no overt indications that he was deeply troubled."[3] Church friends of the twenty-one-year-old distance runner "expected her to win the NCAA championship, not to run away from it. And they never thought this woman would try to end a life so full of promise."[4]

Is the darkness of suicide greater than the light of understanding and prevention? According to experts like Adina Wrobleski, who became a suicidologist after her daughter killed herself in 1979, suicide does not happen without warning and is usually the end of a long process.

"Initially suicide often stuns the people left behind," says Wrobleski, "but as they are able to look back, they often recall clues and warnings. Of any ten persons who kill themselves, eight have given definite warnings of their suicidal intentions. Our society, however, has not taught the public what these clues and warnings are, and what to do when they see them."

Wrobleski believes these clues and warnings are most often associated with a major mental illness, and that little progress will be made in understanding suicide until mental illness is treated as a health problem as serious as heart disease, cancer or AIDS.

Although many authorities agree with Wrobleski, some caution that not all suicidal persons are mentally ill. According to the *Harvard Medical School Mental Health Letter* (February 1986), the most immediate cause of and clue to suicide is despair:

> In one long-term study, hopelessness alone accounted for most of the association between depression and suicide, and a high level of hopelessness was the strongest sign that a person who had attempted suicide would try again. Intense guilt, psychotic delusions, and even the severity of the depression were much less adequate indicators.[5]

Tragically, this hopelessness appears to take its greatest toll on teenagers. Such dark feelings are hard to detect because they are often masked by boredom, apathy, hyperactivity or physical complaints.

In 1984 Don Posterski, Ontario director for InterVarsity Christian Fellowship, conducted an exhaustive cultural analysis of Canadian teenagers. He examined such things as their ethics, values, self-perceptions and views of the future. Over seventy-four per cent of those he talked to saw suicide as a serious or very serious problem for themselves or for their friends.

"I was absolutely stunned by the fact that three-quarters of a youth generation is struggling with this," says Posterski. "An overwhelming majority are wondering whether they are going to survive, whether they will live long enough to die a natural death."

Why are so many teenagers plagued by such dreadful doubts? What causes such unbearable despair?

Some experts believe that the increase in teen suicide is due simply to the increase in the availability of firearms, drugs and alcohol. In 1984 more than eighty per cent of all reported teenage suicides had alcohol in their systems; nearly ninety per cent of all teenagers experimented with alcohol or drugs before age fourteen.[6] Recent studies, however, indicate more complex reasons for teen stress. These include the increase in family breakups, society's greater mobility (which can weaken the extended family) and increased demands on parents (which can make them less available to youngsters).

Stress can affect anyone, even youth who are outwardly successful. The 1986 annual survey, sponsored by Who's Who Among American High School Students, found that thirty-one per cent of high-achieving teenagers have contemplated suicide and four per cent have attempted it. The top five factors the teenagers felt contributed most to suicide were feelings of personal worthlessness, feelings of isolation and loneliness, pressure to achieve, fear of failure, and drug and alcohol use.[7]

At the heart of these factors is something indelibly imprinted into the fabric of society—the pursuit of the American Dream and the good life it promises to all. Some Christian teaching has added an additional burden—the gospel of prosperity that links obedience and faith to obtaining that American dream.

Michal Gorman, a Washington, D.C., psychotherapist, believes that today's American society does little to nurture the spiritual strength of its citizens. Instead, it encourages Americans to value gathering external and material things, especially if they can do it without effort.

Under the auspices of the St. Francis Center, Gorman has taught an eighteen-week course, "Death and Dying, Life and Living" in the Washington, D.C., school system. The teenagers she talks to are aware of problems like nuclear war and the budget deficit. But they have been taught to respond to them not by asking "What more can I do?" but rather by asking "What more can I accumulate?"

"Today's society nurtures a deadly emptiness," says Gorman. "Our national budget, with its emphasis on the military, increases ways to kill people and decreases ways to feed people or to provide them with funds for college. Kids are being forced to live in a society where the guiding image or myth seems to deny everything that feels human, spiritual or compassionate. The pressure for teenagers today is to find a way to live in an environment that feels so empty. Is it any wonder that so many are drinking and taking drugs? I know that if I don't feel that I'm living life in connection with my soul or spirit or whatever makes me human, then everything else is meaningless."

"Most of the responses to teen suicide are centered around the question, What is going on with these kids that they are killing themselves?" says Gorman. "My question is, What are these kids trying to tell us that is so important they're willing to die to do it? My hunch is they're trying to say, 'I can't stand the pressure. Please pay attention to who I am, not to what I have.' "

In his article, "Teen Suicide: Beyond the Mask," author Stephan Ulstein confirms Gorman's perspective. He believes an increasingly violent and materialistic American society is steering young adults away from spiritual values and toward temporal ones that provide little real fulfillment:

As the rich get richer and the poor get poorer in America, the message to kids is, "grab your piece of the pie before it's too late." For those who are unsure of their ability to compete in an increasingly tight job market—or even to get into college—the fear of failure can be overwhelming.[8]

Posterski's study of Canadian adolescents indicated that they, too, have a greater awareness of contemporary social problems than did past generations. At the top of their concerns was the problem of unemployment, followed by drugs, child abuse and nuclear war. More important to them than success and the good life were appreciating friendships and the desire to be loved.

"I'm encouraged in their perspective that says they value people more than they value things," says Posterski. "That is not to say, however, that things are not important to them. What we have to understand about youth is that they do not shape their world. They inherit it. They are the recipients of what we give to them, and it appears that what we have given them is a present existence which raises a lot of questions about their future. We have a generation of young people who will probably have less in the future rather than more. They feel betrayed and are deeply pessimistic."

An inexperienced, emotionally sensitive teen may be like the child who was too innocent to pretend he saw his emperor's new clothes. Teens sometimes can see causes of suicide that adults, blinded by ingrained habits and comfortable lifestyles, may experience but never notice.

Christianity and Suicide

The violent act of suicide is hard enough to deal with from a secular perspective, let alone a Christian one. Some Christians view it as the absolute immoral act—the unforgivable sin—and ask whether a believer who commits suicide was ever really a follower of Christ. In death, is she or he really with the Lord?

Aside from the sixth commandment, "You shall not murder" (Ex 20:13), the Bible provides no direct judgments on suicide. The most well-known biblical accounts of suicide—Samson (Judges 16:28-31), Saul and his armor bearer (1 Samuel 31:1-6) and Judas Iscariot (Matthew 27:3-10)—also shed little light on this moral dilemma.

Theologians such as Augustine and Thomas Aquinas condemned suicide, laying the groundwork for the church in the Middle Ages to outlaw it. Instead of being given a Christian burial, the body of a suicide victim was put on public display, and the family was ostracized and often punished. Such acts served only to reinforce a taboo that persists today, oppressing not only those who struggle with suicide but their families as well.

In his book *Mere Morality,* theologian Lewis Smedes grapples with the moral implications of suicide and concludes:

> Even if people are not destined by their own natures to be suicidal, some are caught in such horrible hopelessness that they are driven to seek escape in the arms of death. If suicide is a tragic wrong more like cancer than murder, perhaps we can do no better than to hold back judgment, prevent it when we can, and weep when we cannot.[9]

Though not everyone would agree suicide is "more like cancer than murder," there is less scriptural support for the belief that it is the ultimate sin. Posterski believes that suicide, like other sins, will be forgiven and equates it to missing God's ultimate best. He says:

> God does not want us to have such a life of despair that we choose to end it by our own hand. But when we gossip, when divorce strikes, when we're greedy, or when we live without the expression of love in our eyes, we are also missing rapport or acceptance with him. It only means that none of us can come to God after death and say, "I deserve to live with you." That includes the person who takes his or her own life.

But even if one believes that suicide cannot

separate a person from the love of Christ, a question still remains: How can Christ's love help a person *avoid* suicide? Until 1975 there were far fewer suicides among teenagers reared in strong religious environments, according to Dr. Stella Pagano, a suicide research expert at the National Committee on Youth Suicide Prevention. Since then, research has pinpointed a disturbing trend upward among young Catholics and orthodox Jews. Although Pagano has no evidence concerning Evangelicals, she suspects the same may be true.

This doesn't mean that faith in Christ has no positive effect. Citing data for the United States between 1954 and 1978, Allan Carlson, president of The Rockford Institute and director of its Center on the Family in America, notes that "a 1 per cent increase in youth church attendance would produce a 1.4 per cent decrease in youth suicide. From this perspective religion and family are not mere options for us; they are necessary if lives are to be saved."[10] Carlson adds, however, that more and more teens are not attending church and suggests that religious groups need to "return to their spiritual roots" rather than succumbing to "the allure of political activism and to theologies shaped by ideological fads."[11]

Posterski cautions that faith distorted by legalism can drive some *deeper* into depression.

"One of my concerns is that too many Christians deny reality as they seek to be perfect," he states. "That is in contrast to the teaching of Christ that said, 'You shall know the truth, and the truth shall set you free.' I wish we could have more integrity in our teaching of our humanity as God chooses to leave it with us. We are earthen vessels transformed in Christ, but still earthen. We make and will always make mistakes. When we deny that, we create hypocrisy and we exert excessive pressure."

What Can the Church Do?

Because someone struggling with suicide will most often seek help from a pastor before a physician or psychiatrist, the church plays a critical role in suicide prevention. In *Responding to Suicidal Crisis,* author Doman Lum notes that warning a person of his or her Christian responsibility not to commit suicide has little effect on the suicidal person. He recommends instead "the love of God manifested in concrete care. Perhaps it is only as the minister and other caring persons incarnate the message of trust and love that the suicide may understand that GOD CARES FOR HIM and that life offers meaningful existence."[12]

To learn such care, Christians will have to educate themselves about suicide. Many have already begun the process. Bill Blake chose to get involved in response to the University of Wisconsin student's death mentioned earlier (the student had attended an InterVarsity conference at which Blake was an InterVarsity staff member). Blake organized and conducted a suicide-and-depression workshop to encourage and train others to become more aware of suicidal students. According to Blake, it is often difficult to discern whether someone is seriously suicidal or mildly depressed:

> We must learn to listen even if we suspect a depressed person is using us to get attention. Never take suicide lightly if someone is talking about it. Approximately seventy-five per cent of the people who kill themselves do so on the first try.

In addition to seeing that the suicidal person receives immediate professional help (from both a medical physician and a therapist or psychiatrist), Blake advises, at the very least, that support groups be formed to uphold and encourage the individual.

In Washington, D.C., Michal Gorman has formed such support groups in high schools so that teenagers will have a safe place, or "holding presence," as she calls it, to question the value of life and to face the possibility of death. Gorman believes strongly that struggling with such issues is a necessary prerequisite to living life fully and with integrity:

23

The moment we are born, we are aware of our mortality on some level. In an age of nuclear weapons, this awareness is even more acute. Kids, and adults for that matter, need a place where they can ask, "Am I going to live or am I going to die? Am I going to seize the possibility of life?" And for Christians, it means asking questions like, "What does it mean that I have to die in order to live in Christ?" Providing a holding presence—and certainly Christ is such a presence—defines the difference between the internal struggle of facing death and the external act of actually choosing it. The presence of caring people allows and nurtures an internal transformation from hopelessness to hope, from powerlessness to power, from questioning life to embracing it. Agreeing that efforts should be made to teach young people to accept their humanness, Don Posterski has developed a "suicide curriculum packet" that he and his staff have distributed to young people in Ontario high schools and colleges. "Suicide is something that happens in slow motion," says Posterski. "A person doesn't wake up Saturday morning and say, 'Life isn't worth living, so I'm going to end it tonight.' Because of that, we have all kinds of opportunities to intercept these people with the hope of Christ."

Suicide-and-depression-workshop organizer Bill Blake would explain it this way: "When someone talks about wanting to die, we need to hear that person's pain and become intimately acquainted with his or her hopelessness. Then we can, with integrity, tell them that Christ stands in the midst of their pain to give life and to give it abundantly." Blake believes that suicide prevention at its core requires embodying the gospel of hope for those who feel hopeless.

The Struggle Continues
The moment I stood up to walk to the medicine cabinet five years ago, I caught sight of my address book sitting on the edge of my desk. I slowly picked up the phone receiver. It felt heavy, like an anchor. I dialed my best friend. She did not answer. I dialed a friend who lived 500 miles away. We talked for three straight hours, stopping only for ten minutes while she reached my best friend.

Charlotte arrived while I was still on the phone. She embraced me and said, "I love you, and Christ will never abandon you." She sat in my desk chair, put me on her lap and held me close as she rocked back and forth whispering, "Christ will never abandon you." I sobbed until I fell asleep. Hours later, I woke up. Charlotte was by my side praying. She placed a cool

25

washcloth on my forehead and whispered, "You aren't alone." I said, "I'm afraid." She replied, "I am, too. But I promise not to leave. Christ will be here in the morning."

That morning I woke up, alive. Charlotte and I established a contract between us whereby I promised to contact her when I wanted to die and she promised to be present in whatever way she could.

Since then, I have worked in many ways to control my suicidal urges. I hold on to Charlotte's commitment to me and get professional help through individual therapy when I think it is needed. I've found a "holding presence" through my church, St. Stephen and the Incarnation, in downtown Washington, D.C. And I find tangible ways to keep myself "tethered" to the earth. I exercise, take piano lessons, paint, pump gas at a local service station and continue to keep a journal. Nurturing a passion for creativity—in any form—has helped to stifle what once was my passion for destruction.

I still ask *Why?* about many things, and I still think about death. Will I ever kill myself? No. My motto in life once was, "Life's a bitch, and then you die." One day I discovered that it had become, "Life's a bitch, and then you live." The discovery came quietly, gently, like the sunrise I once dreaded. Like grace.

Not many know about my struggle with suicide. I know I am not the only Christian to endure such a battle. "For to me, to live is Christ and to die is gain," writes Paul. "If I am to go on living in the body, this will mean fruitful labor for me. Yet what shall I choose? I do not know! I am torn between the two: I desire to depart and be with Christ, which is better by far; but it is more necessary for you that I remain in the body" (Phil 1:21–24).

I read those verses and receive precious solace, knowing that on some level Paul struggled with choosing life over death, life with those around me over life in the presence of Christ. I also receive solace from words that others like myself have written about their struggles with suicide. In my journal, I have recorded this eloquent statement from Karen Kenyon, a woman whose husband killed himself in 1979:

> There are no good answers to the questions of why someone takes his or her own life. All we can do is to pose for ourselves the question of our own being and non-being. The question of existence every day is a real one. Life need not just happen to us. We can choose. We are choosing every moment which direction to turn—toward the light or toward the dark.

Like the writer of those words, I am stronger as a result of my struggle, now able to swallow reality in doses that might suffocate less wounded people. For that, and for the friends who continue to stand with me, I am thankful. Most of all, I am thankful for the face of Christ, which, when I peer directly into the darkness of death, shimmers like a small, warm flame and tenderly beckons my heart once again to choose life. Shine in my heart, Lord Jesus.

Do You or Someone You Know Want to Die?

Answer these questions for yourself or the hurting person you care about:

☐ Have you recently withdrawn from therapeutic help because it's just not worth it and it will never really make a difference?

☐ Have you been abusing drugs or alcohol lately in order to render yourself immune to an overwhelming feeling of despair?

☐ Is there a history of suicide in your family? Do you feel that "the sins of the fathers" have fallen on your shoulders and that killing yourself is the only way to eradicate this "cancer" in your family once and for all?

☐ Are you using a lot of profanity? Are you yelling at people you love? Are you driving your car at high rates of speed, sometimes thinking about how easy it would be to drift into the path of an oncoming truck?

☐ Have you stopped washing your clothes or the dishes? Do you leave bills unopened? Do you look disheveled? Are you showering only once a week?

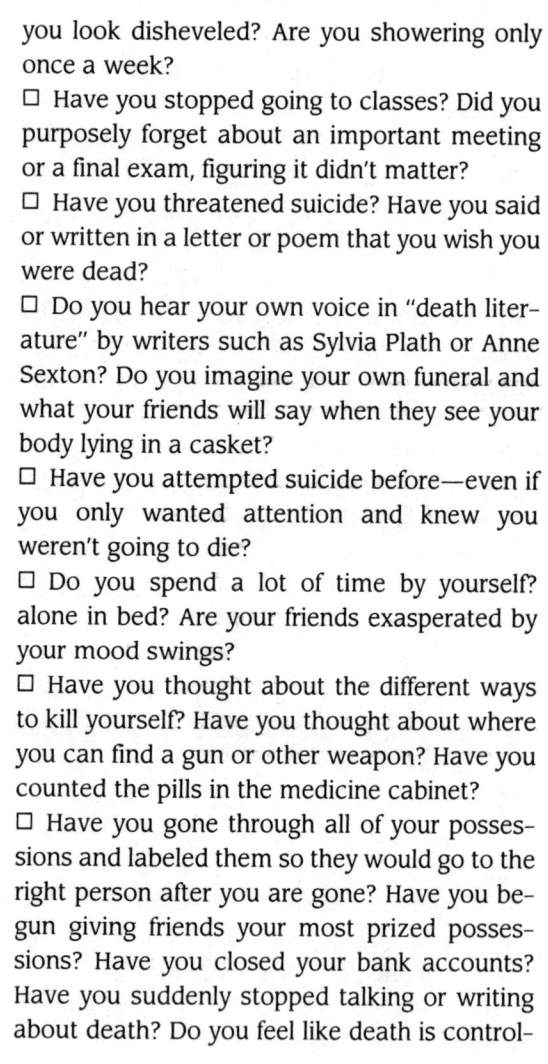

☐ Have you stopped going to classes? Did you purposely forget about an important meeting or a final exam, figuring it didn't matter?

☐ Have you threatened suicide? Have you said or written in a letter or poem that you wish you were dead?

☐ Do you hear your own voice in "death literature" by writers such as Sylvia Plath or Anne Sexton? Do you imagine your own funeral and what your friends will say when they see your body lying in a casket?

☐ Have you attempted suicide before—even if you only wanted attention and knew you weren't going to die?

☐ Do you spend a lot of time by yourself? alone in bed? Are your friends exasperated by your mood swings?

☐ Have you thought about the different ways to kill yourself? Have you thought about where you can find a gun or other weapon? Have you counted the pills in the medicine cabinet?

☐ Have you gone through all of your possessions and labeled them so they would go to the right person after you are gone? Have you begun giving friends your most prized possessions? Have you closed your bank accounts? Have you suddenly stopped talking or writing about death? Do you feel like death is controlling you? Have you written a suicide note?[13]

What to Do If You Are Alone and Thinking about Suicide

☐ Sit down and breathe deeply. Breathe deeply again and again.

☐ Turn on the lights or open a door or window.

☐ Pick up the phone and call a friend, even if you have to call collect. Talk to the operator if you don't have the strength to dial the number.

☐ Say your name out loud. Say your friends' names out loud. Repeat and combine these names with your name.

☐ Cry, even if it means weeping bitterly. Scream: "Lord, God, why am I in such despair? Why did you do this to me? Tell me why."

☐ Pray. Say: "Lord Jesus, help me. Please give me a reason to live."

☐ Touch yourself. Feel the rapid beating of your heart.

☐ Turn on the television, radio or stereo.

☐ Close your eyes and think about *The Wizard of Oz* or chocolate ice cream or giraffes.

☐ Get out a photo album and look at pictures of your family and friends.

☐ If you have a pet, pick it up and hold it tightly.

☐ When you have the strength, get out from where you are. Go to the movies. Go to the shopping mall. Go to a neighbor's or a friend's house. If you are afraid to drive, run as fast as you can for as long as you can. Get yourself to where there are people.

What to Do When Someone Says, "I'm Going to Kill Myself"

☐ Accept what is said, and treat it seriously.

☐ Listen, even if the person is verbally abusing you. Say: "I'm sorry you are in so much pain" or "I will not abandon you."

☐ Embrace or touch the person. Rub his or her back.

☐ Do not give advice and do not say, "Everything will be all right." Say: "I'm asking you not to kill yourself. Please do not kill yourself. My heart will break if you kill yourself."

☐ Do not debate whether suicide is right or wrong. Do not add to the person's guilt by saying, "How can you face God? Think how your parents and friends would feel! How can you be so selfish?"

☐ Help the person recall how he or she used to cope. Ask what the person needs most right now. Food? sleep? money? a hug? answers? Talk openly and freely about the person's intentions. Try to determine whether the person has a plan for suicide—the more detailed the plan, the greater the risk.

☐ Call the police if the situation is immediately life-threatening.

☐ Do not leave the person alone if you believe the risk of suicide is immediate. Trust your suspicions that the person may be self-destructive.

☐ Do not swear you will keep the person's intentions a secret. You may lose a friend, but you may save a life.

☐ Pray for the person silently, saying: "Lord Jesus, you are the source of life. Please graft onto this person's heart a reason to live."[14]

Notes

[1] A. Alvarez, *The Savage God* (New York: Random House, 1970), p. 121.

[2] "For East's Staff, Tragedy and the Task at Hand," *Washington Post*, July 1, 1986.

[3] "Youth's Suicide Raises Anew the Aching Question, 'Why?'" *Washington Post*, June 3, 1986.

[4] "Runner's Plunge Puzzles Friends," *Washington Post*, June 7, 1986.

[5] "Suicide," *Harvard Medical School Mental Health Letter*, February 1986.

[6] John Q. Baucom, *Fatal Choice: The Teenage Suicide Crisis* (Chicago: Moody Press, 1986), p.156.

[7] "High-Achieving Teen-agers Tell of Considering Suicide," *Washington Post*, September 14, 1986.

[8] Stephan Ulstein, "Teen Suicide: Beyond the Mask," *Christian Home and School*, March 1985, p. 11.

[9] Lewis Smedes, *Mere Morality: What God Expects from Ordinary People* (Grand Rapids: Eerdmans, 1983), pp. 112-13.

[10] Allan C. Carlson, "Is There a Teen Suicide Crisis?" *Washington Post*, January 25, 1987.

[11] Ibid.

[12] Doman Lum, *Responding to Suicidal Crisis* (Grand Rap-

ids: Eerdmans, 1974), p. 58.

[13]Adapted from "Suicide Among School Age Youth," December, 1984, State Education Department, University of the State of New York. For more information, contact the National Committee on Youth Suicide Prevention, 666 Fifth Avenue, New York, NY 10103, (212) 957-9292.

[14]Ibid.

Other Helpful Books

Hillman, James. *Suicide and the Soul,* Suffolk: Hodder and Stoughton, 1964.

Shneidman, Edwin S., and Norman C. Farberow. *Clues to Suicide.* New York: McGraw-Hill, 1957.

Also helpful are publications written by Adina Wrobleski. These include "Afterwards," a newsletter about suicide and suicide grief. For more information, contact her at 5124 Grove Street, Minneapolis, MN 55436, (612) 929-6448.

For more information about the facts and myths of mental illness, write for the free booklet, "What You Don't Know about Mental Illness Could Fill a Booklet," from the American Mental Health Fund, Box 17700, Washington, D.C. 20041, (800) 433-5959.

For more information about workshops and/or programs on teen suicide developed by Michal Gorman, write to her at 4707 Connecticut Avenue, N.W., Suite 103, Washington, D.C. 20008, (202) 362-0231.

Letters to the author can be sent c/o InterVarsity Press, 5206 Main Street, P.O. Box 1400, Downers Grove, IL 60515.